A Dog of Flanders

Louisa de la Ramê

AKA Óuida

Alpha Editions

This edition published in 2021

ISBN : 9789355111777

Design and Setting By
Alpha Editions
www.alphaedis.com
Email - info@alphaedis.com

A DOG OF FLANDERS

Nello and Patrasche were left all alone in the world.

They were friends in a friendship closer than brotherhood. Nello was a little Ardennois—Patrasche was a big Fleming. They were both of the same age by length of years, yet one was still young, and the other was already old. They had dwelt together almost all their days: both were orphaned and destitute, and owed their lives to the same hand. It had been the beginning of the tie between them, their first bond of sympathy; and it had strengthened day by day, and had grown with their growth, firm and indissoluble, until they loved one another very greatly. Their home was a little hut on the edge of a little village—a Flemish village a league from Antwerp, set amidst flat breadths of pasture and corn-lands, with long lines of poplars and of alders bending in the breeze on the edge of the great canal which ran through it. It had about a score of houses and homesteads, with shutters of bright green or sky-blue, and roofs rose-red or black and white, and walls white-washed until they shone in the sun like snow. In the centre of the village stood a windmill, placed on a little moss-grown slope: it was a landmark to all the level country round. It had once been painted scarlet, sails and all, but that had been in its infancy, half a century or more earlier, when it had ground wheat for the soldiers of Napoleon; and it was now a ruddy brown, tanned by wind and weather. It went queerly by fits and starts, as though rheumatic and stiff in the joints from age, but it served the whole neighborhood, which would have thought it almost as impious to carry grain elsewhere as to attend any other religious service than the mass that was performed at the altar of the little old gray church, with its conical steeple, which stood opposite to it, and whose single bell rang morning, noon, and night with that strange, subdued, hollow sadness which every bell that hangs in the Low Countries seems to gain as an integral part of its melody.

Within sound of the little melancholy clock almost from their birth upward, they had dwelt together, Nello and Patrasche, in the little hut on the edge of the village, with the cathedral spire of Antwerp rising in the north-east, beyond the great green plain of seeding grass and spreading corn that stretched away from them like a tideless, changeless sea. It was the hut of a very old man, of a very poor man—of old Jehan Daas, who in his time had been a soldier, and who remembered the wars that had trampled the country as oxen tread down the furrows, and who had brought from his service nothing except a wound, which had made him a cripple.

When old Jehan Daas had reached his full eighty, his daughter had died in the Ardennes, hard by Stavelot, and had left him in legacy her two-year-old son. The old man could ill contrive to support himself, but he took up the additional burden uncomplainingly, and it soon became welcome and precious to him. Little Nello—which was but a pet diminutive for Nicolas—throve with him, and the old man and the little child lived in the poor little hut contentedly.

It was a very humble little mud-hut indeed, but it was clean and white as a sea-shell, and stood in a small plot of garden-ground that yielded beans and herbs and pumpkins. They were very poor, terribly poor—many a day they had nothing at all to eat. They never by any chance had enough: to have had enough to eat would have been to have reached paradise at once. But the old man was very gentle and good to the boy, and the boy was a beautiful, innocent, truthful, tender-hearted creature; and they were happy on a crust and a few leaves of cabbage, and asked no more of earth or heaven; save indeed that Patrasche should be always with them, since without Patrasche where would they have been?

For Patrasche was their alpha and omega; their treasury and granary; their store of gold and wand of wealth; their bread-winner and minister; their only friend and comforter. Patrasche dead or gone from them, they must have laid themselves down and died likewise. Patrasche was body, brains, hands, head, and feet to both of them: Patrasche was their very life, their very soul. For Jehan Daas was old and a cripple, and Nello was but a child; and Patrasche was their dog.

{Illustration}

A dog of Flanders—yellow of hide, large of head and limb, with wolf-like ears that stood erect, and legs bowed and feet widened in the muscular development wrought in his breed by many generations of hard service. Patrasche came of a race which had toiled hard and cruelly from sire to son in Flanders many a century—slaves of slaves, dogs of the people, beasts of the shafts and the harness, creatures that lived straining their sinews in the gall of the cart, and died breaking their hearts on the flints of the streets.

Patrasche had been born of parents who had labored hard all their days over the sharp-set stones of the various cities and the long, shadowless, weary roads of the two Flanders and of Brabant. He had been born to no other heritage than those of pain and of toil. He had been fed on curses and baptized with blows. Why not? It was a Christian country, and Patrasche was but a dog. Before he was fully grown he had known the bitter gall of the cart and the collar. Before he had entered his thirteenth month he had become the property of a hardware-dealer, who was accustomed to wander over the land north and south, from the blue sea to the green mountains. They sold him for a small price, because he was so young.

This man was a drunkard and a brute. The life of Patrasche was a life of hell. To deal the tortures of hell on the animal creation is a way which the Christians have of showing their belief in it. His purchaser was a sullen, ill-living, brutal Brabantois, who heaped his cart full with pots and pans and flagons and buckets, and other wares of crockery and brass and tin, and left Patrasche to draw the load as best he might, whilst he himself lounged idly by the side in fat and sluggish ease, smoking his black pipe and stopping at every wineshop or café on the road.

Happily for Patrasche—or unhappily—he was very strong: he came of an iron race, long born and bred to such cruel travail; so that he did not die, but managed to drag on a wretched existence under the brutal burdens, the scarifying lashes, the hunger, the thirst, the blows, the curses, and the exhaustion which are the only wages with which the Flemings repay the most patient and laborious of all their four-footed victims. One day, after two years of this long and deadly agony, Patrasche was going on as usual along one of the straight, dusty, unlovely roads that lead to the city of Rubens. It was full midsummer, and very warm. His cart was very heavy, piled high with goods in metal and in earthenware. His owner sauntered on without noticing him otherwise than by the crack of the whip as it curled round his quivering loins. The Brabantois had paused to drink beer himself at every wayside house, but he had forbidden Patrasche to stop a moment for a draught from the canal. Going along thus, in the full sun, on a scorching highway, having eaten nothing for twenty-four hours, and, which was far worse to him, not having tasted water for near twelve, being blind with dust, sore with blows, and stupefied with the merciless weight which dragged upon his loins, Patrasche staggered and foamed a little at the mouth, and fell.

He fell in the middle of the white, dusty road, in the full glare of the sun; he was sick unto death, and motionless. His master gave him the only medicine in his pharmacy—kicks and oaths and blows with a cudgel of oak, which had been often the only food and drink, the only wage and reward, ever offered to him. But Patrasche was beyond the reach of any torture or of any curses. Patrasche lay, dead to all appearances, down in the white powder of the summer dust. After a while, finding it useless to assail his ribs with punishment and his ears with maledictions, the Brabantois—deeming life gone in him, or going so nearly that his carcass was forever useless, unless indeed some one should strip it of the skin for gloves—cursed him fiercely in farewell, struck off the leathern bands of the harness, kicked his body aside into the grass, and, groaning and muttering in savage wrath, pushed the cart lazily along the road up-hill, and left the dying dog for the ants to sting and for the crows to pick.

It was the last day before Kermesse away at Louvain, and the Brabantois was in haste to reach the fair and get a good place for his truck of brass wares. He was in fierce wrath, because Patrasche had been a strong and much-enduring animal, and because he himself had now the hard task of pushing his charette all the way to Louvain. But to stay to look after Patrasche never entered his thoughts: the beast was dying and useless, and he would steal, to replace him, the first large dog that he found wandering alone out of sight of its master. Patrasche had cost him nothing, or next to nothing, and for two long, cruel years had made him toil ceaselessly in his service from sunrise to sunset, through summer and winter, in fair weather and foul.

He had got a fair use and a good profit out of Patrasche: being human, he was wise, and left the dog to draw his last breath alone in the ditch, and have his bloodshot eyes plucked out as they might be by the birds, whilst he himself went on his way to beg and to steal, to eat and to drink, to dance and to sing, in the mirth at Louvain. A dying dog, a dog of the cart—why should he waste hours over its agonies at peril of losing a handful of copper coins, at peril of a shout of laughter?

Patrasche lay there, flung in the grass-green ditch. It was a busy road that day, and hundreds of people, on foot and on mules, in wagons or in carts, went by, tramping quickly and joyously on to Louvain. Some saw him, most did not even look: all passed on. A dead dog more or less—it was nothing in Brabant: it would be nothing anywhere in the world.

{Illustration}

After a time, among the holiday-makers, there came a little old man who was bent and lame, and very feeble. He was in no guise for feasting: he was very poorly and miserably clad, and he dragged his silent way slowly through the dust among the pleasure-seekers. He looked at Patrasche, paused, wondered, turned aside, then kneeled down in the rank grass and weeds of the ditch, and surveyed the dog with kindly eyes of pity. There was with him a little rosy, fair- haired, dark-eyed child of a few years old, who pattered in amidst the bushes, for him breast-high, and stood gazing with a pretty seriousness upon the poor, great, quiet beast.

Thus it was that these two first met—the little Nello and the big Patrasche.

The upshot of that day was, that old Jehan Daas, with much laborious effort, drew the sufferer homeward to his own little hut, which was a stone's throw off amidst the fields, and there tended him with so much care that the sickness, which had been a brain seizure, brought on by heat and thirst and exhaustion, with time and shade and rest passed away, and health and strength returned, and Patrasche staggered up again upon his four stout, tawny legs.

Now for many weeks he had been useless, powerless, sore, near to death; but all this time he had heard no rough word, had felt no harsh touch, but only the pitying murmurs of the child's voice and the soothing caress of the old man's hand.

In his sickness they too had grown to care for him, this lonely man and the little happy child. He had a corner of the hut, with a heap of dry grass for his bed; and they had learned to listen eagerly for his breathing in the dark night, to tell them that he lived; and when he first was well enough to essay a loud, hollow, broken bay, they laughed aloud, and almost wept together for joy at such a sign of his sure restoration; and little Nello, in delighted glee, hung round his rugged neck with chains of marguerites, and kissed him with fresh and ruddy lips.

So then, when Patrasche arose, himself again, strong, big, gaunt, powerful, his great wistful eyes had a gentle astonishment in them that there were no curses to rouse him and no blows to drive him; and his heart awakened to a mighty love, which never wavered once in its fidelity whilst life abode with him.

But Patrasche, being a dog, was grateful. Patrasche lay pondering long with grave, tender, musing brown eyes, watching the movements of his friends.

Now, the old soldier, Jehan Daas, could do nothing for his living but limp about a little with a small cart, with which he carried daily the milk-cans of those happier neighbors who owned cattle away into the town of Antwerp. The villagers gave him the employment a little out of charity—more because it suited them well to send their milk into the town by so honest a carrier, and bide at home themselves to look after their gardens, their cows, their poultry, or their little fields. But it was becoming hard work for the old man. He was eighty-three, and Antwerp was a good league off, or more.

Patrasche watched the milk-cans come and go that one day when he had got well and was lying in the sun with the wreath of marguerites round his tawny neck.

The next morning, Patrasche, before the old man had touched the cart, arose and walked to it and placed himself betwixt its handles, and testified as plainly as dumb show could do his desire and his ability to work in return for the bread of charity that he had eaten. Jehan Daas resisted long, for the old man was one of those who thought it a foul shame to bind dogs to labor for which Nature never formed them. But Patrasche would not be gainsaid: finding they did not harness him, he tried to draw the cart onward with his teeth.

At length Jehan Daas gave way, vanquished by the persistence and the gratitude of this creature whom he had succored. He fashioned his cart so that Patrasche could run in it, and this he did every morning of his life thenceforward.

When the winter came, Jehan Daas thanked the blessed fortune that had brought him to the dying dog in the ditch that fair-day of Louvain; for he was very old, and he grew feebler with each year, and he would ill have known how to pull his load of milk-cans over the snows and through the deep ruts in the mud if it had not been for the strength and the industry of the animal he had befriended. As for Patrasche, it seemed heaven to him. After the frightful burdens that his old master had compelled him to strain under, at the call of the whip at every step, it seemed nothing to him but amusement to step out with this little light green cart, with its bright brass cans, by the side of the gentle old man who always paid him with a tender caress and with a kindly word. Besides, his work was over by three or four in the day, and after that time he was free to do as he would—to stretch himself, to sleep in the sun, to wander in the fields, to romp with the young child, or to play with his fellow-dogs. Patrasche was very happy.

Fortunately for his peace, his former owner was killed in a drunken brawl at the Kermesse of Mechlin, and so sought not after him nor disturbed him in his new and well-loved home.

{Illustration}

{Illustration}

A few years later, old Jehan Daas, who had always been a cripple, became so paralyzed with rheumatism that it was impossible for him to go out with the cart any more. Then little Nello, being now grown to his sixth year of age, and knowing the town well from having accompanied his grandfather so many times, took his place beside the cart, and sold the milk and received the coins in exchange, and brought them back to their respective owners with a pretty grace and seriousness which charmed all who beheld him.

The little Ardennois was a beautiful child, with dark, grave, tender eyes, and a lovely bloom upon his face, and fair locks that clustered to his throat; and many an artist sketched the group as it went by him—the green cart with the brass flagons of Teniers and Mieris and Van Tal, and the great tawny-colored, massive dog, with his belled harness that chimed cheerily as he went, and the small figure that ran beside him which had little white feet in great wooden shoes, and a soft, grave, innocent, happy face like the little fair children of Rubens.

Nello and Patrasche did the work so well and so joyfully together that Jehan Daas himself, when the summer came and he was better again, had no need to stir out, but could sit in the doorway in the sun and see them go forth through the garden wicket, and then doze and dream and pray a little, and then awake again as the clock tolled three and watch for their return. And on their return Patrasche would shake himself free of his harness with a bay of glee, and Nello would recount with pride the doings of the day; and they would all go in together to their meal of rye bread and milk or soup, and would see the shadows lengthen over the great plain, and see the twilight veil the fair cathedral spire; and then lie down together to sleep peacefully while the old man said a prayer. So the days and the years went on, and the lives of Nello and Patrasche were happy, innocent, and healthful. In the spring and summer especially were they glad. Flanders is not a lovely land, and around the burgh of Rubens it is perhaps least lovely of all. Corn and colza, pasture and plough, succeed each other on the characterless plain in wearying repetition, and save by some gaunt gray tower, with its peal of pathetic bells, or some figure coming athwart the fields, made picturesque by a gleaner's bundle or a woodman's fagot, there is no change, no variety, no beauty anywhere; and he who has dwelt upon the mountains or amidst the forests feels oppressed as by imprisonment with the tedium and the endlessness of that vast and dreary level. But it is green and very fertile, and it has wide horizons that have a certain charm of their own even in their dulness and monotony; and among the rushes by the water-side the flowers grow, and the trees rise tall and fresh where the barges glide with their great hulks black against the sun, and their little green barrels and vari-colored flags gay against the leaves. Anyway, there is greenery and breadth of space enough to be as good as beauty to a child and a dog; and these two asked no better, when their work was done, than to lie buried in the lush grasses on the side of the canal, and watch the cumbrous vessels drifting by and bring the crisp salt smell of the sea among the blossoming scents of the country summer.

True, in the winter it was harder, and they had to rise in the darkness and the bitter cold, and they had seldom as much as they could have eaten any day, and the hut was scarce better than a shed when the nights were cold, although it looked so pretty in warm weather, buried in a great kindly clambering vine, that never bore fruit, indeed, but which covered it with luxuriant green tracery all through the months of blossom and harvest. In winter the winds found many holes in the walls of the poor little hut, and the vine was black and leafless, and the bare lands looked very bleak and drear without, and sometimes within the floor was flooded and then frozen. In winter it was hard, and the snow numbed the little white limbs of Nello, and the icicles cut the brave, untiring feet of Patrasche.

But even then they were never heard to lament, either of them. The child's wooden shoes and the dog's four legs would trot manfully together over the frozen fields to the chime of the bells on the harness; and then sometimes, in the streets of Antwerp, some housewife would bring them a bowl of soup and a handful of bread, or some kindly trader would throw some billets of fuel into the little cart as it went homeward, or some woman in their own village would bid them keep a share of the milk they carried for their own food; and they would run over the white lands, through the early darkness, bright and happy, and burst with a shout of joy into their home.

So, on the whole, it was well with them, very well; and Patrasche, meeting on the highway or in the public streets the many dogs who toiled from daybreak into nightfall, paid only with blows and curses, and loosened from the shafts with a kick to starve and freeze as best they might—Patrasche in his heart was very grateful to his fate, and thought it the fairest and the kindliest the world could hold. Though he was often very hungry indeed when he lay down at night; though he had to work in the heats of summer noons and the rasping chills of winter dawns; though his feet were often tender with wounds from the sharp edges of the jagged pavement; though he had to perform tasks beyond his strength and against his nature—yet he was grateful and content: he did his duty with each day, and the eyes that he loved smiled down on him. It was sufficient for Patrasche.

{Illustration}

There was only one thing which caused Patrasche any uneasiness in his life, and it was this. Antwerp, as all the world knows, is full at every turn of old piles of stones, dark and ancient and majestic, standing in crooked courts, jammed against gateways and taverns, rising by the water's edge, with bells ringing above them in the air, and ever and again out of their arched doors a swell of music pealing. There they remain, the grand old sanctuaries of the past, shut in amidst the squalor, the hurry, the crowds, the unloveliness, and the commerce of the modern world, and all day long the clouds drift and the birds circle and the winds sigh around them, and beneath the earth at their feet there sleeps—RUBENS.

And the greatness of the mighty Master still rests upon Antwerp, and wherever we turn in its narrow streets his glory lies therein, so that all mean things are thereby transfigured; and as we pace slowly through the winding ways, and by the edge of the stagnant water, and through the noisome courts, his spirit abides with us, and the heroic beauty of his visions is about us, and the stones that once felt his footsteps and bore his shadow seem to arise and speak of him with living voices. For the city which is the tomb of Rubens still lives to us through him, and him alone.

It is so quiet there by that great white sepulchre—so quiet, save only when the organ peals and the choir cries aloud the Salve Regina or the Kyrie Eleison. Sure no artist ever had a greater gravestone than that pure marble sanctuary gives to him in the heart of his birthplace in the chancel of St. Jacques.

Without Rubens, what were Antwerp? A dirty, dusky, bustling mart, which no man would ever care to look upon save the traders who do business on its wharves. With Rubens, to the whole world of men it is a sacred name, a sacred soil, a Bethlehem where a god of Art saw light, a Golgotha where a god of Art lies dead.

O nations! closely should you treasure your great men, for by them alone will the future know of you. Flanders in her generations has been wise. In his life she glorified this greatest of her sons, and in his death she magnifies his name. But her wisdom is very rare.

Now, the trouble of Patrasche was this. Into these great, sad piles of stones, that reared their melancholy majesty above the crowded roofs, the child Nello would many and many a time enter, and disappear through their dark arched portals, whilst Patrasche, left without upon the pavement, would wearily and vainly ponder on what could be the charm which thus allured from him his inseparable and beloved companion. Once or twice he did essay to see for himself, clattering up the steps with his milk-cart behind him; but thereon he had been always sent back again summarily by a tall custodian in black clothes and silver chains of office; and fearful of bringing his little master into trouble, he desisted, and remained couched patiently before the churches until such time as the boy reappeared. It was not the fact of his going into them which disturbed Patrasche: he knew that people went to church: all the village went to the small, tumbledown, gray pile opposite the red windmill.

What troubled him was that little Nello always looked strangely when he came out, always very flushed or very pale; and whenever he returned home after such visitations would sit silent and dreaming, not caring to play, but gazing out at the evening skies beyond the line of the canal, very subdued and almost sad.

What was it? wondered Patrasche. He thought it could not be good or natural for the little lad to be so grave, and in his dumb fashion he tried all he could to keep Nello by him in the sunny fields or in the busy marketplace. But to the churches Nello would go: most often of all would he go to the great cathedral; and Patrasche, left without on the stones by the iron fragments of Quentin Matsys's gate, would stretch himself and yawn and sigh, and even howl now and then, all in vain, until the doors closed and the child perforce came forth again, and winding his arms about the dog's neck would kiss him on his broad, tawney-colored forehead, and murmur always the same words: "If I could only see them, Patrasche!—if I could only see them!"

What were they? pondered Patrasche, looking up with large, wistful, sympathetic eyes.

One day, when the custodian was out of the way and the doors left ajar, he got in for a moment after his little friend and saw. "They" were two great covered pictures on either side of the choir.

Nello was kneeling, rapt as in an ecstasy, before the altar-picture of the Assumption, and when he noticed Patrasche, and rose and drew the dog gently out into the air, his face was wet with tears, and he looked up at the veiled places as he passed them, and murmured to his companion, "It is so terrible not to see them, Patrasche, just because one is poor and cannot pay! He never meant that the poor should not see them when he painted them, I am sure. He would have had us see them any day, every day: that I am sure. And they keep them shrouded there—shrouded in the dark, the beautiful things!— and they never feel the light, and no eyes look on them, unless rich people come and pay. If I could only see them, I would be content to die."

But he could not see them, and Patrasche could not help him, for to gain the silver piece that the church exacts as the price for looking on the glories of the Elevation of the Cross and the Descent of the Cross was a thing as utterly beyond the powers of either of them as it would have been to scale the heights of the cathedral spire. They had never so much as a sou to spare: if they cleared enough to get a little wood for the stove, a little broth for the pot, it was the utmost they could do. And yet the heart of the child was set in sore and endless longing upon beholding the greatness of the two veiled Rubens.

{Illustration: tree} {Illustration: scenery}

The whole soul of the little Ardennois thrilled and stirred with an absorbing passion for Art. Going on his ways through the old city in the early days before the sun or the people had risen, Nello, who looked only a little peasant-boy, with a great dog drawing milk to sell from door to door, was in a heaven of dreams whereof Rubens was the god. Nello, cold and hungry, with stockingless feet in wooden shoes, and the winter winds blowing among his curls and lifting his poor thin garments, was in a rapture of meditation, wherein all that he saw was the beautiful fair face of the Mary of the Assumption, with the waves of her golden hair lying upon her shoulders, and the light of an eternal sun shining down upon her brow. Nello, reared in poverty, and buffeted by fortune, and untaught in letters, and unheeded by men, had the compensation or the curse which is called Genius.

No one knew it. He as little as any. No one knew it. Only indeed Patrasche, who, being with him always, saw him draw with chalk upon the stones any and every thing that grew or breathed, heard him on his little bed of hay murmur all manner of timid, pathetic prayers to the spirit of the great Master; watched his gaze darken and his face radiate at the evening glow of sunset or the rosy rising of the dawn; and felt many and many a time the tears of a strange, nameless pain and joy, mingled together, fall hotly from the bright young eyes upon his own wrinkled yellow forehead.

"I should go to my grave quite content if I thought, Nello, that when thou growest a man thou couldst own this hut and the little plot of ground, and labor for thyself, and be called Baas by thy neighbors," said the old man Jehan many an hour from his bed. For to own a bit of soil, and to be called Baas—master—by the hamlet round, is to have achieved the highest ideal of a Flemish peasant; and the old soldier, who had wandered over all the earth in his youth, and had brought nothing back, deemed in his old age that to live and die on one spot in contented humility was the fairest fate he could desire for his darling. But Nello said nothing.

The same leaven was working in him that in other times begat Rubens and Jordaens and the Van Eycks, and all their wondrous tribe, and in times more recent begat in the green country of the Ardennes, where the Meuse washes the old walls of Dijon, the great artist of the Patroclus, whose genius is too near us for us aright to measure its divinity.

Nello dreamed of other things in the future than of tilling the little rood of earth, and living under the wattle roof, and being called Baas by neighbors a little poorer or a little less poor than himself. The cathedral spire, where it rose beyond the fields in the ruddy evening skies or in the dim, gray, misty mornings, said other things to him than this. But these he told only to Patrasche, whispering, childlike, his fancies in the dog's ear when they went together at their work through the fogs of the daybreak, or lay together at their rest among the rustling rushes by the water's side.

For such dreams are not easily shaped into speech to awake the slow sympathies of human auditors; and they would only have sorely perplexed and troubled the poor old man bedridden in his corner, who, for his part, whenever he had trodden the streets of Antwerp, had thought the daub of blue and red that they called a Madonna, on the walls of the wine-shop where he drank his sou's worth of black beer, quite as good as any of the famous altar-pieces for which the stranger folk travelled far and wide into Flanders from every land on which the good sun shone.

There was only one other beside Patrasche to whom Nello could talk at all of his daring fantasies. This other was little Alois, who lived at the old red mill on the grassy mound, and whose father, the miller, was the best-to-do husbandman in all the village. Little Alois was only a pretty baby with soft round, rosy features, made lovely by those sweet dark eyes that the Spanish rule has left in so many a Flemish face, in testimony of the Alvan dominion, as Spanish art has left broadsown throughout the country majestic palaces and stately courts, gilded house-fronts and sculptured lintels— histories in blazonry and poems in stone.

Little Alois was often with Nello and Patrasche. They played in the fields, they ran in the snow, they gathered the daisies and bilberries, they went up to the old gray church together, and they often sat together by the broad wood-fire in the mill-house. Little Alois, indeed, was the richest child in the hamlet. She had neither brother nor sister; her blue serge dress had never a hole in it; at Kermesse she had as many gilded nuts and Agni Dei in sugar as her hands could hold; and when she went up for her first communion her flaxen curls were covered with a cap of richest Mechlin lace, which had been her mother's and her grandmother's before it came to her. Men spoke already, though she had but twelve years, of the good wife she would be for their sons to woo and win; but she herself was a little gay, simple child, in nowise conscious of her heritage, and she loved no playfellows so well as Jehan Daas's grandson and his dog.

{Illustration: child} {Illustration: NELLO DREW THEIR LIKENESS WITH A STICK OF CHARCOAL} {Illustration: couple walking}

One day her father, Baas Cogez, a good man, but somewhat stern, came on a pretty group in the long meadow behind the mill, where the aftermath had that day been cut. It was his little daughter sitting amidst the hay, with the great tawny head of Patrasche on her lap, and many wreaths of poppies and blue corn-flowers round them both: on a clean smooth slab of pine wood the boy Nello drew their likeness with a stick of charcoal.

The miller stood and looked at the portrait with tears in his eyes, it was so strangely like, and he loved his only child closely and well. Then he roughly chid the little girl for idling there whilst her mother needed her within, and sent her indoors crying and afraid: then, turning, he snatched the wood from Nello's hands. "Dost do much of such folly?" he asked, but there was a tremble in his voice.

Nello colored and hung his head. "I draw everything I see," he murmured.

The miller was silent: then he stretched his hand out with a franc in it. "It is folly, as I say, and evil waste of time: nevertheless, it is like Alois, and will please the house-mother. Take this silver bit for it and leave it for me."

The color died out of the face of the young Ardennois; he lifted his head and put his hands behind his back. "Keep your money and the portrait both, Baas Cogez," he said, simply. "You have been often good to me." Then he called Patrasche to him, and walked away across the field.

"I could have seen them with that franc," he murmured to Patrasche, "but I could not sell her picture—not even for them."

Baas Cogez went into his mill-house sore troubled in his mind. "That lad must not be so much with Alois," he said to his wife that night. "Trouble may come of it hereafter: he is fifteen now, and she is twelve; and the boy is comely of face and form."

"And he is a good lad and a loyal," said the housewife, feasting her eyes on the piece of pine wood where it was throned above the chimney with a cuckoo clock in oak and a Calvary in wax.

"Yea, I do not gainsay that," said the miller, draining his pewter flagon.

"Then, if what you think of were ever to come to pass," said the wife, hesitatingly, "would it matter so much? She will have enough for both, and one cannot be better than happy."

"You are a woman, and therefore a fool," said the miller, harshly, striking his pipe on the table. "The lad is naught but a beggar, and, with these painter's fancies, worse than a beggar. Have a care that they are not together in the future, or I will send the child to the surer keeping of the nuns of the Sacred Heart."

The poor mother was terrified, and promised humbly to do his will. Not that she could bring herself altogether to separate the child from her favorite playmate, nor did the miller even desire that extreme of cruelty to a young lad who was guilty of nothing except poverty. But there were many ways in which little Alois was kept away from her chosen companion; and Nello, being a boy proud and quiet and sensitive, was quickly wounded, and ceased to turn his own steps and those of Patrasche, as he had been used to do with every moment of leisure, to the old red mill upon the slope. What his offence was he did not know: he supposed he had in some manner angered Baas Cogez by taking the portrait of Alois in the meadow; and when the child who loved him would run to him and nestle her hand in his, he would smile at her very sadly and say with a tender concern for her before himself, "Nay, Alois, do not anger your father. He thinks that I make you idle, dear, and he is not pleased that you should be with me. He is a good man and loves you well: we will not anger him, Alois."

But it was with a sad heart that he said it, and the earth did not look so bright to him as it had used to do when he went out at sunrise under the poplars down the straight roads with Patrasche. The old red mill had been a landmark to him, and he had been used to pause by it, going and coming, for a cheery greeting with its people as her little flaxen head rose above the low mill-wicket, and her little rosy hands had held out a bone or a crust to Patrasche. Now the dog looked wistfully at a closed door, and the boy went on without pausing, with a pang at his heart, and the child sat within with tears dropping slowly on the knitting to which she was set on her little stool by the stove; and Baas Cogez, working among his sacks and his mill-gear, would harden his will and say to himself, "It is best so. The lad is all but a beggar, and full of idle, dreaming fooleries. Who knows what mischief might not come of it in the future?" So he was wise in his generation, and would not have the door unbarred, except upon rare and formal occasion, which seemed to have neither warmth nor mirth in them to the two children, who had been accustomed so long to a daily gleeful, careless, happy interchange of greeting, speech, and pastime, with no other watcher of their sports or auditor of their fancies than Patrasche, sagely shaking the brazen bells of his collar and responding with all a dog's swift sympathies to their every change of mood.

All this while the little panel of pine wood remained over the chimney in the mill-kitchen with the cuckoo clock and the waxen Calvary, and sometimes it seemed to Nello a little hard that whilst his gift was accepted he himself should be denied.

{Illustration: }

But he did not complain: it was his habit to be quiet: old Jehan Daas had said ever to him, "We are poor: we must take what God sends—the ill with the good: the poor cannot choose."

To which the boy had always listened in silence, being reverent of his old grandfather; but nevertheless a certain vague, sweet hope, such as beguiles the children of genius, had whispered in his heart, "Yet the poor do choose sometimes—choose to be great, so that men cannot say them nay." And he thought so still in his innocence; and one day, when the little Alois, finding him by chance alone among the cornfields by the canal, ran to him and held him close, and sobbed piteously because the morrow would be her saint's day, and for the first time in all her life her parents had failed to bid him to the little supper and romp in the great barns with which her feast-day was always celebrated, Nello had kissed her and murmured to her in firm faith,

"It shall be different one day, Alois. One day that little bit of pine wood that your father has of mine shall be worth its weight in silver; and he will not shut the door against me then. Only love me always, dear little Alois, only love me always, and I will be great."

"And if I do not love you?" the pretty child asked, pouting a little through her tears, and moved by the instinctive coquetries of her sex.

Nello's eyes left her face and wandered to the distance, where in the red and gold of the Flemish night the cathedral spire rose. There was a smile on his face so sweet and yet so sad that little Alois was awed by it. "I will be great still," he said under his breath—"great still, or die, Alois."

"You do not love me," said the little spoilt child, pushing him away; but the boy shook his head and smiled, and went on his way through the tall yellow corn, seeing as in a vision some day in a fair future when he should come into that old familiar land and ask Alois of her people, and be not refused or denied, but received in honor, whilst the village folk should throng to look upon him and say in one another's ears, "Dost see him? He is a king among men, for he is a great artist and the world speaks his name; and yet he was only our poor little Nello, who was a beggar as one may say, and only got his bread by the help of his dog." And he thought how he would fold his grandsire in furs and purples, and portray him as the old man is portrayed in the Family in the chapel of St. Jacques; and of how he would hang the throat of Patrasche with a collar of gold, and place him on his right hand, and say to the people, "This was once my only friend;" and of how he would build himself a great white marble palace, and make to himself luxuriant gardens of pleasure, on the slope looking outward to where the cathedral spire rose, and not dwell in it himself, but summon to it, as to a home, all men young and poor and friendless, but of the will to do mighty things; and of how he would say to them always, if they sought to bless his name, "Nay, do not thank me—thank Rubens. Without him, what should I have been?" And these dreams, beautiful, impossible, innocent, free of all selfishness, full of heroical worship, were so closely about him as he went that he was happy—happy even on this sad anniversary of Alois's saint's day, when he and Patrasche went home by themselves to the little dark hut and the meal of black bread, whilst in the mill-house all the children of the village sang and laughed, and ate the big round cakes of Dijon and the almond gingerbread of Brabant, and danced in the great barn to the light of the stars and the music of flute and fiddle.

"Never mind, Patrasche," he said, with his arms round the dog's neck as they both sat in the door of the hut, where the sounds of the mirth at the mill came down to them on the night air—"never mind. It shall all be changed by and by."

He believed in the future: Patrasche, of more experience and of more philosophy, thought that the loss of the mill supper in the present was ill compensated by dreams of milk and honey in some vague hereafter. And Patrasche growled whenever he passed by Baas Cogez.

"This is Alois's name-day, is it not?" said the old man Daas that night from the corner where he was stretched upon his bed of sacking.

The boy gave a gesture of assent: he wished that the old man's memory had erred a little, instead of keeping such sure account.

"And why not there?" his grandfather pursued. "Thou hast never missed a year before, Nello."

"Thou art too sick to leave," murmured the lad, bending his handsome head over the bed.

"Tut! tut! Mother Nulette would have come and sat with me, as she does scores of times. What is the cause, Nello?" the old man persisted. "Thou surely hast not had ill words with the little one?"

"Nay, grandfather—never," said the boy quickly, with a hot color in his bent face. "Simply and truly, Baas Cogez did not have me asked this year. He has taken some whim against me."

"But thou hast done nothing wrong?"

"That I know—nothing. I took the portrait of Alois on a piece of pine: that is all."

"Ah!" The old man was silent: the truth suggested itself to him with the boy's innocent answer. He was tied to a bed of dried leaves in the corner of a wattle hut, but he had not wholly forgotten what the ways of the world were like.

He drew Nello's fair head fondly to his breast with a tenderer gesture. "Thou art very poor, my child," he said with a quiver the more in his aged, trembling voice—"so poor! It is very hard for thee."

"Nay, I am rich," murmured Nello; and in his innocence he thought so—rich with the imperishable powers that are mightier than the might of kings. And he went and stood by the door of the hut in the quiet autumn night, and watched the stars troop by and the tall poplars bend and shiver in the wind. All the casements of the mill- house were lighted, and every now and then the notes of the flute came to him. The tears fell down his cheeks, for he was but a child, yet he smiled, for he said to himself, "In the future!" He stayed there until all was quite still and dark, then he and Patrasche went within and slept together, long and deeply, side by side.

{Illustration}

Now he had a secret which only Patrasche knew. There was a little outhouse to the hut, which no one entered but himself—a dreary place, but with abundant clear light from the north. Here he had fashioned himself rudely an easel in rough lumber, and here on a great gray sea of stretched paper he had given shape to one of the innumerable fancies which possessed his brain. No one had ever taught him anything; colors he had no means to buy; he had gone without bread many a time to procure even the few rude vehicles that he had here; and it was only in black or white that he could fashion the things he saw. This great figure which he had drawn here in chalk was only an old man sitting on a fallen tree—only that.

He had seen old Michel the woodman sitting so at evening many a time. He had never had a soul to tell him of outline or perspective, of anatomy or of shadow, and yet he had given all the weary, worn- out age, all the sad, quiet patience, all the rugged, careworn pathos of his original, and given them so that the old lonely figure was a poem, sitting there, meditative and alone, on the dead tree, with the darkness of the descending night behind him.

It was rude, of course, in a way, and had many faults, no doubt; and yet it was real, true in nature, true in art, and very mournful, and in a manner beautiful.

Patrasche had lain quiet countless hours watching its gradual creation after the labor of each day was done, and he knew that Nello had a hope—vain and wild perhaps, but strongly cherished—of sending this great drawing to compete for a prize of two hundred francs a year which it was announced in Antwerp would be open to every lad of talent, scholar or peasant, under eighteen, who would attempt to win it with some unaided work of chalk or pencil. Three of the foremost artists in the town of Rubens were to be the judges and elect the victor according to his merits.

All the spring and summer and autumn Nello had been at work upon this treasure, which, if triumphant, would build him his first step toward independence and the mysteries of the art which he blindly, ignorantly, and yet passionately adored.

He said nothing to any one: his grandfather would not have understood, and little Alois was lost to him. Only to Patrasche he told all, and whispered, "Rubens would give it me, I think, if he knew."

Patrasche thought so too, for he knew that Rubens had loved dogs or he had never painted them with such exquisite fidelity; and men who loved dogs were, as Patrasche knew, always pitiful.

The drawings were to go in on the first day of December, and the decision be given on the twenty-fourth, so that he who should win might rejoice with all his people at the Christmas season.

In the twilight of a bitter wintry day, and with a beating heart, now quick with hope, now faint with fear, Nello placed the great picture on his little green milk-cart, and took it, with the help of Patrasche, into the town, and there left it, as enjoined, at the doors of a public building.

"Perhaps it is worth nothing at all. How can I tell?" he thought, with the heart-sickness of a great timidity. Now that he had left it there, it seemed to him so hazardous, so vain, so foolish, to dream that he, a little lad with bare feet, who barely knew his letters, could do anything at which great painters, real artists, could ever deign to look. Yet he took heart as he went by the cathedral: the lordly form of Rubens seemed to rise from the fog and the darkness, and to loom in its magnificence before him, whilst the lips, with their kindly smile, seemed to him to murmur, "Nay, have courage! It was not by a weak heart and by faint fears that I wrote my name for all time upon Antwerp."

Nello ran home through the cold night, comforted. He had done his best: the rest must be as God willed, he thought, in that innocent, unquestioning faith which had been taught him in the little gray chapel among the willows and the poplar-trees.

{Illustration: }

The winter was very sharp already. That night, after they reached the hut, snow fell; and fell for very many days after that, so that the paths and the divisions in the fields were all obliterated, and all the smaller streams were frozen over, and the cold was intense upon the plains. Then, indeed, it became hard work to go round for the milk while the world was all dark, and carry it through the darkness to the silent town. Hard work, especially for Patrasche, for the passage of the years, that were only bringing Nello a stronger youth, were bringing him old age, and his joints were stiff and his bones ached often. But he would never give up his share of the labor. Nello would fain have spared him and drawn the cart himself, but Patrasche would not allow it. All he would ever permit or accept was the help of a thrust from behind to the truck as it lumbered along through the ice-ruts. Patrasche had lived in harness, and he was proud of it. He suffered a great deal sometimes from frost, and the terrible roads, and the rheumatic pains of his limbs, but he only drew his breath hard and bent his stout neck, and trod onward with steady patience.

"Rest thee at home, Patrasche—it is time thou didst rest—and I can quite well push in the cart by myself," urged Nello many a morning; but

Patrasche, who understood him aright, would no more have consented to stay at home than a veteran soldier to shirk when the charge was sounding; and every day he would rise and place himself in his shafts, and plod along over the snow through the fields that his four round feet had left their print upon so many, many years.

"One must never rest till one dies," thought Patrasche; and sometimes it seemed to him that that time of rest for him was not very far off. His sight was less clear than it had been, and it gave him pain to rise after the night's sleep, though he would never lie a moment in his straw when once the bell of the chapel tolling five let him know that the daybreak of labor had begun.

"My poor Patrasche, we shall soon lie quiet together, you and I," said old Jehan Daas, stretching out to stroke the head of Patrasche with the old withered hand which had always shared with him its one poor crust of bread; and the hearts of the old man and the old dog ached together with one thought: When they were gone, who would care for their darling?

One afternoon, as they came back from Antwerp over the snow, which had become hard and smooth as marble over all the Flemish plains, they found dropped in the road a pretty little puppet, a tambourine- -player, all scarlet and gold, about six inches high, and, unlike greater personages when Fortune lets them drop, quite unspoiled and unhurt by its fall. It was a pretty toy. Nello tried to find its owner, and, failing, thought that it was just the thing to please Alois.

It was quite night when he passed the mill-house: he knew the little window of her room. It could be no harm, he thought, if he gave her his little piece of treasure-trove, they had been playfellows so long. There was a shed with a sloping roof beneath her casement: he climbed it and tapped softly at the lattice: there was a little light within. The child opened it and looked out half frightened. Nello put the tambourine-player into her hands. "Here is a doll I found in the snow, Alois. Take it," he whispered—"take it, and God bless thee, dear!"

He slid down from the shed-roof before she had time to thank him, and ran off through the darkness.

That night there was a fire at the mill. Outbuildings and much corn were destroyed, although the mill itself and the dwelling-house were unharmed. All the village was out in terror, and engines came tearing through the snow from Antwerp. The miller was insured, and would lose nothing: nevertheless, he was in furious wrath, and declared aloud that the fire was due to no accident, but to some foul intent.

Nello, awakened from his sleep, ran to help with the rest: Baas Cogez thrust him angrily aside. "Thou wert loitering here after dark," he said roughly. "I believe, on my soul, that thou dost know more of the fire than any one."

Nello heard him in silence, stupefied, not supposing that any one could say such things except in jest, and not comprehending how any one could pass a jest at such a time.

Nevertheless, the miller said the brutal thing openly to many of his neighbors in the day that followed; and though no serious charge was ever preferred against the lad, it got bruited about that Nello had been seen in the mill-yard after dark on some unspoken errand, and that he bore Baas Cogez a grudge for forbidding his intercourse with little Alois; and so the hamlet, which followed the sayings of its richest landowner servilely, and whose families all hoped to secure the riches of Alois in some future time for their sons, took the hint to give grave looks and cold words to old Jehan Daas's grandson. No one said anything to him openly, but all the village agreed together to humor the miller's prejudice, and at the cottages and farms where Nello and Patrasche called every morning for the milk for Antwerp, downcast glances and brief phrases replaced to them the broad smiles and cheerful greetings to which they had been always used. No one really credited the miller's absurd suspicion, nor the outrageous accusations born of them, but the people were all very poor and very ignorant, and the one rich man of the place had pronounced against him. Nello, in his innocence and his friendlessness, had no strength to stem the popular tide.

"Thou art very cruel to the lad," the miller's wife dared to say, weeping, to her lord. "Sure he is an innocent lad and a faithful, and would never dream of any such wickedness, however sore his heart might be."

But Baas Cogez being an obstinate man, having once said a thing held to it doggedly, though in his innermost soul he knew well the injustice that he was committing.

Meanwhile, Nello endured the injury done against him with a certain proud patience that disdained to complain: he only gave way a little when he was quite alone with old Patrasche. Besides, he thought, "If it should win! They will be sorry then, perhaps."

Still, to a boy not quite sixteen, and who had dwelt in one little world all his short life, and in his childhood had been caressed and applauded on all sides, it was a hard trial to have the whole of that little world turn against him for naught. Especially hard in that bleak, snow-bound, famine-stricken winter-time, when the only light and warmth there could be found abode beside the village hearths and in the kindly greetings of neighbors. In the winter-time all drew nearer to each other, all to all, except to Nello and Patrasche, with whom none now would have anything to do, and who were left to fare as they might with the old paralyzed, bedridden man in the little cabin, whose fire was often low, and whose board was often without bread, for there was a buyer from Antwerp who had taken to drive his mule in of a day for the milk of the various dairies, and there were only three or four of the people who had refused his terms of purchase and remained faithful to the little green cart. So that the burden which Patrasche drew had become very light, and the centime-pieces in Nello's pouch had become, alas! very small likewise.

The dog would stop, as usual, at all the familiar gates, which were now closed to him, and look up at them with wistful, mute appeal; and it cost the neighbors a pang to shut their doors and their hearts, and let Patrasche draw his cart on again, empty. Nevertheless, they did it, for they desired to please Baas Cogez.

Noël was close at hand.

The weather was very wild and cold. The snow was six feet deep, and the ice was firm enough to bear oxen and men upon it everywhere. At this season the little village was always gay and cheerful. At the poorest dwelling there were possets and cakes, joking and dancing, sugared saints and gilded Jésus. The merry Flemish bells jingled everywhere on the horses; everywhere within doors some well-filled soup-pot sang and smoked over the stove; and everywhere over the snow without laughing maidens pattered in bright kerchiefs and stout kirtles, going to and from the mass. Only in the little hut it was very dark and very cold.

Nello and Patrasche were left utterly alone, for one night in the week before the Christmas Day, Death entered there, and took away from life forever old Jehan Daas, who had never known life aught save its poverty and its pains. He had long been half dead, incapable of any movement except a feeble gesture, and powerless for anything beyond a gentle word; and yet his loss fell on them both with a great horror in it: they mourned him passionately. He had passed away from them in his sleep, and when in the gray dawn they learned their bereavement, unutterable solitude and desolation seemed to close around them. He had long been only a poor, feeble, paralyzed old man, who could not raise a hand in their defence, but he had loved them well: his smile had always welcomed their return. They mourned for him unceasingly, refusing to be comforted, as in the white winter day they followed the deal shell that held his body to the nameless grave by the little gray church. They were his only mourners, these two whom he had left friendless upon earth—the young boy and the old dog.

"Surely, he will relent now and let the poor lad come hither?" thought the miller's wife, glancing at her husband smoking by the hearth.

Baas Cogez knew her thought, but he hardened his heart, and would not unbar his door as the little, humble funeral went by. "The boy is a beggar," he said to himself: "he shall not be about Alois."

The woman dared not say anything aloud, but when the grave was closed and the mourners had gone, she put a wreath of immortelles into Alois's hands and bade her go and lay it reverently on the dark, unmarked mound where the snow was displaced.

Nello and Patrasche went home with broken hearts. But even of that poor, melancholy, cheerless home they were denied the consolation. There was a month's rent over-due for their little home, and when Nello had paid the last sad service to the dead he had not a coin left. He went and begged grace of the owner of the hut, a cobbler who went every Sunday night to drink his pint of wine and smoke with Baas Cogez. The cobbler would grant no mercy. He was a harsh, miserly man, and loved money. He claimed in default of his rent every stick and stone, every pot and pan, in the hut, and bade Nello and Patrasche be out of it on the morrow.

Now, the cabin was lowly enough, and in some sense miserable enough, and yet their hearts clove to it with a great affection. They had been so happy there, and in the summer, with its clambering vine and its flowering beans, it was so pretty and bright in the midst of the sunlighted fields! There life in it had been full of labor and privation, and yet they had been so well content, so gay of heart, running together to meet the old man's never-failing smile of welcome!

All night long the boy and the dog sat by the fireless hearth in the darkness, drawn close together for warmth and sorrow. Their bodies were insensible to the cold, but their hearts seemed frozen in them.

When the morning broke over the white, chill earth it was the morning of Christmas Eve. With a shudder, Nello clasped close to him his only friend, while his tears fell hot and fast on the dog's frank forehead. "Let us go, Patrasche—dear, dear Patrasche," he murmured. "We will not wait to be kicked out: let us go."

Patrasche had no will but his, and they went sadly, side by side, out from the little place which was so dear to them both, and in which every humble, homely thing was to them precious and beloved. Patrasche drooped his head wearily as he passed by his own green cart: it was no longer his—it had to go with the rest to pay the rent, and his brass harness lay idle and glittering on the snow. The dog could have lain down beside it and died for very heart-sickness as he went, but whilst the lad lived and needed him Patrasche would not yield and give way.

They took the old accustomed road into Antwerp. The day had yet scarce more than dawned, most of the shutters were still closed, but some of the villagers were about. They took no notice whilst the dog and the boy passed by them. At one door Nello paused and looked wistfully within: his grandfather had done many a kindly turn in neighbor's service to the people who dwelt there.

"Would you give Patrasche a crust?" he said, timidly. "He is old, and he has had nothing since last forenoon."

The woman shut the door hastily, murmuring some vague saying about wheat and rye being very dear that season. The boy and the dog went on again wearily: they asked no more.

By slow and painful ways they reached Antwerp as the chimes tolled ten.

"If I had anything about me I could sell to get him bread!" thought Nello, but he had nothing except the wisp of linen and serge that covered him, and his pair of wooden shoes. Patrasche understood, and nestled his nose into the lad's hand, as though to pray him not to be disquieted for any woe or want of his.

The winner of the drawing-prize was to be proclaimed at noon, and to the public building where he had left his treasure Nello made his way. On the steps and in the entrance-hall there was a crowd of youths—some of his age, some older, all with parents or relatives or friends. His heart was sick with fear as he went among them, holding Patrasche close to him. The great bells of the city clashed out the hour of noon with brazen clamor. The doors of the inner hall were opened; the eager, panting throng rushed in: it was known that the selected picture would be raised above the rest upon a wooden dais..

A mist obscured Nello's sight, his head swam, his limbs almost failed him. When his vision cleared he saw the drawing raised on high: it was not his own! A slow, sonorous voice was proclaiming aloud that victory had been adjudged to Stephen Kiesslinger, born in the burgh of Antwerp, son of a wharfinger in that town.

When Nello recovered his consciousness he was lying on the stones without, and Patrasche was trying with every art he knew to call him back to life. In the distance a throng of the youths of Antwerp were shouting around their successful comrade, and escorting him with acclamations to his home upon the quay.

The boy staggered to his feet and drew the dog into his embrace. "It is all over, dear Patrasche," he murmured—"all over!"

He rallied himself as best he could, for he was weak from fasting, and retraced his steps to the village. Patrasche paced by his side with his head drooping and his old limbs feeble from hunger and sorrow.

The snow was falling fast: a keen hurricane blew from the north: it was bitter as death on the plains. It took them long to traverse the familiar path, and the bells were sounding four of the clock as they approached the hamlet. Suddenly Patrasche paused, arrested by a scent in the snow, scratched, whined, and drew out with his teeth a small case of brown leather. He held it up to Nello in the darkness. Where they were there stood a little Calvary, and a lamp burned dully under the cross: the boy mechanically turned the case to the light: on it was the name of Baas Cogez, and within it were notes for two thousand francs.

The sight roused the lad a little from his stupor. He thrust it in his shirt, and stroked Patrasche and drew him onward. The dog looked up wistfully in his face.

Nello made straight for the mill-house, and went to the house-door and struck on its panels. The miller's wife opened it weeping, with little Alois clinging close to her skirts. "Is it thee, thou poor lad?" she said kindly through her tears. "Get thee gone ere the Baas see thee. We are in sore trouble to-night. He is out seeking for a power of money that he has let fall riding homeward, and in this snow he never will find it; and God knows it will go nigh to ruin us. It is Heaven's own judgment for the things we have done to thee."

Nello put the note-case in her hand and called Patrasche within the house. "Patrasche found the money to-night," he said quickly. "Tell Baas Cogez so: I think he will not deny the dog shelter and food in his old age. Keep him from pursuing me, and I pray of you to be good to him."

Ere either woman or dog knew what he meant he had stooped and kissed Patrasche: then closed the door hurriedly, and disappeared in the gloom of the fast—falling night.

The woman and the child stood speechless with joy and fear: Patrasche vainly spent the fury of his anguish against the iron- bound oak of the barred house-door. They did not dare unbar the door and let him forth: they tried all they could to solace him. They brought him sweet cakes and juicy meats; they tempted him with the best they had; they tried to lure him to abide by the warmth of the hearth; but it was of no avail. Patrasche refused to be comforted or to stir from the barred portal.

It was six o'clock when from an opposite entrance the miller at last came, jaded and broken, into his wife's presence. "It is lost forever," he said, with an ashen cheek and a quiver in his stern voice. "We have looked with lanterns everywhere: it is gone—the little maiden's portion and all!"

His wife put the money into his hand, and told him how it had come to her. The strong man sank trembling into a seat and covered his face, ashamed and almost afraid. "I have been cruel to the lad," he muttered at length: "I deserved not to have good at his hands."

Little Alois, taking courage, crept close to her father and nestled against him her fair curly head. "Nello may come here again, father?" she whispered. "He may come to-morrow as he used to do?"

The miller pressed her in his arms: his hard, sunburned face was very pale and his mouth trembled. "Surely, surely," he answered his child. "He shall bide here on Christmas Day, and any other day he will. God helping me, I will make amends to the boy—I will make amends."

Little Alois kissed him in gratitude and joy, then slid from his knees and ran to where the dog kept watch by the door. "And to-night I may feast Patrasche?" she cried in a child's thoughtless glee.

Her father bent his head gravely: "Ay, ay: let the dog have the best;" for the stern old man was moved and shaken to his heart's depths.

It was Christmas Eve, and the mill-house was filled with oak logs and squares of turf, with cream and honey, with meat and bread, and the rafters were hung with wreaths of evergreen, and the Calvary and the cuckoo clock looked out from a mass of holly. There were little paper lanterns, too, for Alois, and toys of various fashions and sweetmeats in bright-pictured papers. There were light and warmth and abundance everywhere, and the child would fain have made the dog a guest honored and feasted.

But Patrasche would neither lie in the warmth nor share in the cheer. Famished he was and very cold, but without Nello he would partake neither of comfort nor food. Against all temptation he was proof, and close against the door he leaned always, watching only for a means of escape.

"He wants the lad," said Baas Cogez. "Good dog! good dog! I will go over to the lad the first thing at day-dawn." For no one but Patrasche knew that Nello had left the hut, and no one but Patrasche divined that Nello had gone to face starvation and misery alone.

The mill-kitchen was very warm: great logs crackled and flamed on the hearth; neighbors came in for a glass of wine and a slice of the fat goose baking for supper. Alois, gleeful and sure of her playmate back on the morrow, bounded and sang and tossed back her yellow hair. Baas Cogez, in the fulness of his heart, smiled on her through moistened eyes, and spoke of the way in which he would befriend her favorite companion; the house-mother sat with calm, contented face at the spinning-wheel; the cuckoo in the clock chirped mirthful hours. Amidst it all Patrasche was bidden with a thousand words of welcome to tarry there a cherished guest. But neither peace nor plenty could allure him where Nello was not.

When the supper smoked on the board, and the voices were loudest and gladdest, and the Christ-child brought choicest gifts to Alois, Patrasche, watching always an occasion, glided out when the door was unlatched by a careless new-comer, and as swiftly as his weak and tired limbs would bear him sped over the snow in the bitter, black night. He had only one thought—to follow Nello. A human friend might have paused for the pleasant meal, the cheery warmth, the cosey slumber; but that was not the friendship of Patrasche. He remembered a bygone time, when an old man and a little child had found him sick unto death in the wayside ditch.

Snow had fallen freshly all the evening long; it was now nearly ten; the trail of the boy's footsteps was almost obliterated. It took Patrasche long to discover any scent. When at last he found it, it was lost again quickly, and lost and recovered, and again lost and again recovered, a hundred times or more.

The night was very wild. The lamps under the wayside crosses were blown out; the roads were sheets of ice; the impenetrable darkness hid every trace of habitations; there was no living thing abroad. All the cattle were housed, and in all the huts and homesteads men and women rejoiced and feasted. There was only Patrasche out in the cruel cold—old and famished and full of pain, but with the strength and the patience of a great love to sustain him in his search.

The trail of Nello's steps, faint and obscure as it was under the new snow, went straightly along the accustomed tracks into Antwerp. It was past midnight when Patrasche traced it over the boundaries of the town and into the narrow, tortuous, gloomy streets. It was all quite dark in the town, save where some light gleamed ruddily through the crevices of house-shutters, or some group went homeward with lanterns chanting drinking-songs. The streets were all white with ice: the high walls and roofs loomed black against them. There was scarce a sound save the riot of the winds down the passages as they tossed the creaking signs and shook the tall lamp-irons.

{Illustration: The portals of the cathedral were unclosed after the Midnight Mass}

So many passers-by had trodden through and through the snow, so many diverse paths had crossed and recrossed each other, that the dog had a hard task to retain any hold on the track he followed. But he kept on his way, though the cold pierced him to the bone, and the jagged ice cut his feet, and the hunger in his body gnawed like a rat's teeth. He kept on his way, a poor gaunt, shivering thing, and by long patience traced the steps he loved into the very heart of the burgh and up to the steps of the great cathedral.

"He is gone to the things that he loved," thought Patrasche: he could not understand, but he was full of sorrow and of pity for the art-passion that to him was so incomprehensible and yet so sacred.

The portals of the cathedral were unclosed after the midnight mass. Some heedlessness in the custodians, too eager to go home and feast or sleep, or too drowsy to know whether they turned the keys aright, had left one of the doors unlocked. By that accident the foot-falls Patrasche sought had passed through into the building, leaving the white marks of snow upon the dark stone floor. By that slender white thread, frozen as it fell, he was guided through the intense silence, through the immensity of the vaulted space—guided straight to the gates of the chancel, and, stretched there upon the stones, he found Nello. He crept up and touched the face of the boy. "Didst thou dream that I should be faithless and forsake thee? I—a dog?" said that mute caress.

The lad raised himself with a low cry and clasped him close. "Let us lie down and die together," he murmured. "Men have no need of us, and we are all alone."

In answer, Patrasche crept closer yet, and laid his head upon the young boy's breast. The great tears stood in his brown, sad eyes: not for himself—for himself he was happy.

They lay close together in the piercing cold. The blasts that blew over the Flemish dikes from the northern seas were like waves of ice, which froze every living thing they touched. The interior of the immense vault of stone in which they were was even more bitterly chill than the snow-covered plains without. Now and then a bat moved in the shadows—now and then a gleam of light came on the ranks of carven figures. Under the Rubens they lay together quite still, and soothed almost into a dreaming slumber by the numbing narcotic of the cold. Together they dreamed of the old glad days when they had chased each other through the flowering grasses of the summer meadows, or sat hidden in the tall bulrushes by the water's side, watching the boats go seaward in the sun.

Suddenly through the darkness a great white radiance streamed through the vastness of the aisles; the moon, that was at her height, had broken through the clouds, the snow had ceased to fall, the light reflected from the snow without was clear as the light of dawn. It fell through the arches full upon the two pictures above, from which the boy on his entrance had flung back the veil: the Elevation and the Descent of the Cross were for one instant visible.

Nello rose to his feet and stretched his arms to them; the tears of a passionate ecstasy glistened on the paleness of his face. "I have seen them at last!" he cried aloud. "O God, it is enough!"

His limbs failed under him, and he sank upon his knees, still gazing upward at the majesty that he adored. For a few brief moments the light illumined the divine visions that had been denied to him so long—light clear and sweet and strong as though it streamed from the throne of Heaven. Then suddenly it passed away: once more a great darkness covered the face of Christ.

The arms of the boy drew close again the body of the dog. "We shall see His face—*there,*" he murmured; "and He will not part us, I think." On the morrow, by the chancel of the cathedral, the people of Antwerp found them both. They were both dead: the cold of the night had frozen into stillness alike the young life and the old. When the Christmas morning broke and the priests came to the temple, they saw them lying thus on the stones together. Above the veils were drawn back from the great visions of Rubens, and the fresh rays of the sunrise touched the thorn-crowned head of the Christ.

As the day grew on there came an old, hard-featured man who wept as women weep. "I was cruel to the lad," he muttered, "and now I would have made amends—yea, to the half of my substance—and he should have been to me as a son."

There came also, as the day grew apace, a painter who had fame in the world, and who was liberal of hand and of spirit. "I seek one who should have had the prize yesterday had worth won," he said to the people—"a boy of rare promise and genius. An old wood-cutter on a fallen tree at eventide—that was all his theme. But there was greatness for the future in it. I would fain find him, and take him with me and teach him Art."

And a little child with curling fair hair, sobbing bitterly as she clung to her father's arm, cried aloud, "Oh, Nello, come! We have all ready for thee. The Christ-child's hands are full of gifts, and the old piper will play for us; and the mother says thou shalt stay by the hearth and burn nuts with us all the Noël week long—yes, even to the Feast of the Kings! And Patrasche will be so happy! Oh, Nello, wake and come!"

But the young pale face, turned upward to the light of the great Rubens with a smile upon its mouth, answered them all, "It is too late."

For the sweet, sonorous bells went ringing through the frost, and the sunlight shone upon the plains of snow, and the populace trooped gay and glad through the streets, but Nello and Patrasche no more asked charity at their hands. All they needed now Antwerp gave unbidden.

Death had been more pitiful to them than longer life would have been. It had taken the one in the loyalty of love, and the other in the innocence of faith, from a world which for love has no recompense and for faith no fulfilment.

All their lives they had been together, and in their deaths they were not divided: for when they were found the arms of the boy were folded too closely around the dog to be severed without violence, and the people of their little village, contrite and ashamed, implored a special grace for them, and, making them one grave, laid them to rest there side by side—forever!